# My PREGNANCY Journal

Nina Štajner

# There's a baby on the way!

## Celebrating the story of Baby's beginning

I first knew I was pregnant when ................................................................

Where I was at the time ................................................................

................................................................

The first person I told was ................................................................

................................................................

What they said ................................................................

................................................................

................................................................

Due date

................................................................

My first thoughts and feelings

............................................................
............................................................
............................................................
............................................................
............................................................
............................................................
............................................................
............................................................
............................................................
............................................................

'You were made perfectly to be loved.'
– Elizabeth Barrett Browning

# First trimester

During the first trimester, a single cell develops into a baby-shaped bundle with tiny fingers and toes.

My first pregnancy symptoms were ....................................................
..........................................................................................
..........................................................................................

My favourite food is .......................................................................

My favourite smells are ...................................................................

I am craving ..............................................................................

I expect pregnancy will be ................................................................
..........................................................................................

# JOURNAL OF WEEKS 1–12

Things I want to remember about these weeks

..............................................................................................

..............................................................................................

..............................................................................................

..............................................................................................

..............................................................................................

..............................................................................................

..............................................................................................

..............................................................................................

..............................................................................................

By the end of the first trimester, Baby is about the size of a lemon.

Our first scan

Scan date

........................................

My current pregnancy symptoms are ...............................................................
................................................................................................................
................................................................................................................

At the first scan I saw ..................................................................................
................................................................................................................
................................................................................................................

I am most nervous about ..............................................................................

I am most excited about ...............................................................................
................................................................................................................
................................................................................................................

# All about Baby

Baby is still growing, but there is already a lot to know.

Possible names

..................................................................................

..................................................................................

..................................................................................

..................................................................................

..................................................................................

Our first nicknames for Baby

..................................................................................

..................................................................................

..................................................................................

..................................................................................

My thoughts about finding out the baby's sex

..........................................................................................

..........................................................................................

..........................................................................................

Sounds Baby hears every day

..........................................................................................

..........................................................................................

..........................................................................................

Songs I sing or play to Baby

..........................................................................................

..........................................................................................

..........................................................................................

# Second trimester

In the second trimester, Baby starts to move and kick.

My current pregnancy symptoms are ..............................................................

..............................................................................................................

..............................................................................................................

My favourite thing about being pregnant is ...................................................

..............................................................................................................

During this trimester, I plan to ....................................................................

..............................................................................................................

..............................................................................................................

..............................................................................................................

..............................................................................................................

# JOURNAL OF WEEKS 13–27

Things I want to remember about these weeks

# Getting to know you

Baby can now hear voices and other sounds.
Parents-to-be get to see their baby again at a second scan.

Our second scan

At the second scan I saw

..................................................
..................................................
..................................................
..................................................
..................................................
..................................................

I realised

..................................................
..................................................
..................................................
..................................................
..................................................
..................................................

I learned that ..........................................................................................

..................................................................................................................

..................................................................................................................

How I felt ..................................................................................................

..................................................................................................................

..................................................................................................................

# Changing and growing

By the end of the second trimester, Baby is the size of an aubergine!

The most surprising thing about pregnancy is

………………………………………………………………………………

………………………………………………………………………………

………………………………………………………………………………

………………………………………………………………………………

………………………………………………………………………………

………………………………………………………………………………

………………………………………………………………………………

………………………………………………………………………………

………………………………………………………………………………

………………………………………………………………………………

………………………………………………………………………………

………………………………………………………………………………

New symptoms and cravings

..................................................................................

..................................................................................

..................................................................................

..................................................................................

..................................................................................

..................................................................................

The best thing about this trimester is

..................................................................................

..................................................................................

..................................................................................

'I love thee, Baby! For thine own sweet sake.'

– Percy Bysshe Shelley

# Being pregnant

Your body is growing a new human being.
That's amazing!

My favourite way to relax is ............................................................

................................................................................................

................................................................................................

My self-care routine is ...................................................................

................................................................................................

................................................................................................

My favourite maternity outfit is .....................................................

................................................................................................

My favourite sleeping position is ...................................................

................................................................................................

A photograph from the second trimester

# Making plans

There are lots of things for parents-to-be to think about.

Where Baby will be born

..................................................................................

..................................................................................

I predict my baby will arrive on

..................................................................................

..................................................................................

### PREDICTIONS MADE BY OTHER SPECIAL PEOPLE!

| Name | Predicted birth date |
| --- | --- |
| .......................................... | .......................................... |
| .......................................... | .......................................... |
| .......................................... | .......................................... |

My birth plan

..................................................................

..................................................................

..................................................................

..................................................................

Things to do before Baby arrives

..................................................................

..................................................................

..................................................................

..................................................................

..................................................................

..................................................................

..................................................................

# Third trimester

In the third trimester, Baby's body and brain are maturing and growing.

My current pregnancy symptoms are ....................................................
................................................................................
................................................................................

Baby is busiest when ................................................................
................................................................................

The most helpful thing I've learned so far is ........................
................................................................................
................................................................................
................................................................................

# JOURNAL OF WEEKS 28–40

Things I want to remember about these weeks

# Baby will soon be here

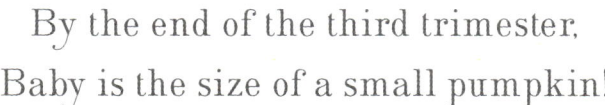

By the end of the third trimester,
Baby is the size of a small pumpkin!

Things I'm doing to prepare ......................................................
..............................................................................................
..............................................................................................

Things I have bought for Baby ..................................................
..............................................................................................
..............................................................................................

How I'm sleeping .......................................................................
..............................................................................................
..............................................................................................

Most vivid dream .......................................................................
..............................................................................................
..............................................................................................

A photograph from the third trimester

# Family and friends

Lots of people will be excited to meet the new arrival.

| Special family members | What they would like to be called |
| --- | --- |
| .................................. | .................................. |
| .................................. | .................................. |
| .................................. | .................................. |
| .................................. | .................................. |
| .................................. | .................................. |
| .................................. | .................................. |
| .................................. | .................................. |

Other people who will be important in Baby's life

..................................................

..................................................

..................................................

Pets my baby will play with

..................................................
..................................................
..................................................
..................................................
..................................................
..................................................

Places we will visit together

..................................................
..................................................
..................................................
..................................................
..................................................
..................................................

Traditions I want to share with Baby

..................................................................................................................
..................................................................................................................
..................................................................................................................
..................................................................................................................
..................................................................................................................

*'Increase of love brings increase of happiness.'*
— Anne Brontë

# Getting ready

It's nearly time for Baby to arrive!

I am most looking forward to

......................................................................................................

......................................................................................................

The person or people who will support me during the birth

......................................................................................................

......................................................................................................

The first people my baby will meet

......................................................................................................

......................................................................................................

......................................................................................................

......................................................................................................

Things I will need for my hospital bag (or for Baby's birth)

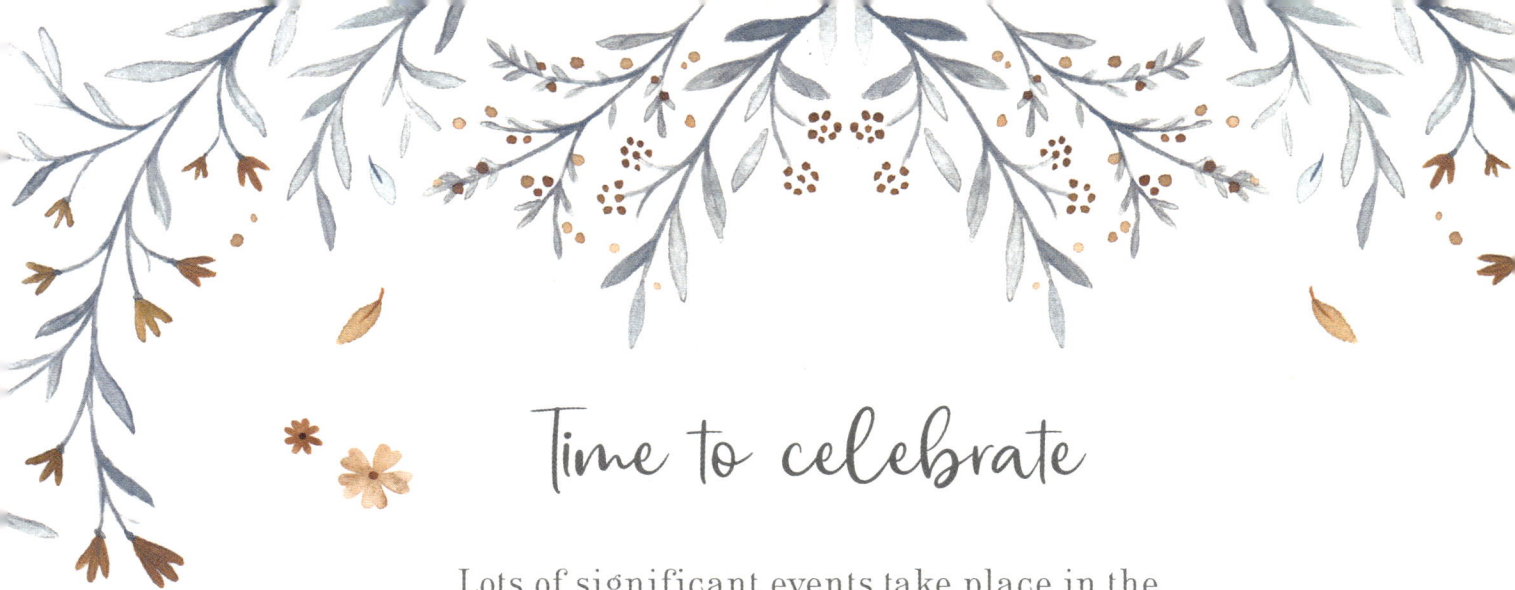

## Time to celebrate

Lots of significant events take place in the nine months before Baby arrives.

Special occasions that happened during my pregnancy ......................
................................................................
................................................................

The people we celebrated with ................................................
................................................................
................................................................

Special gifts I received ................................................
................................................................
................................................................

My happiest moment was ................................................

Favourite memories

# Nearly there!

It has been an incredible nine months waiting for your new baby.

The nicest thing about being pregnant

..................................................................................................

..................................................................................................

..................................................................................................

..................................................................................................

The most memorable moments

..................................................................................................

..................................................................................................

..................................................................................................

..................................................................................................

People who helped make it special

........................................................................................................

........................................................................................................

........................................................................................................

........................................................................................................

The best pieces of advice I received during my pregnancy

........................................................................................................

........................................................................................................

........................................................................................................

........................................................................................................

# The years to come

Things I want to share with my baby

.....................................................................................................

.....................................................................................................

.....................................................................................................

.....................................................................................................

Milestones I am looking forward to

.....................................................................................................

.....................................................................................................

.....................................................................................................

.....................................................................................................